BIGGEST NAMES IN SPORTS

BROOKS KOEPKA

by Anthony K. Hewson

GOLF STAR

FOCUS
READERS.
NAVIGATOR

WWW.FOCUSREADERS.COM

Focus Readers is distributed by North Star Editions:
sales@northstareditions.com | 888-417-0195

Produced for Focus Readers by Red Line Editorial.

Photographs ©: Gregory Vasil/Cal Sport Media/AP Images, cover, 1, 22–23; Charlie Riedel/AP Images, 4–5, 7; Chris Carlson/AP Images, 9; Darren Carroll/Sports Illustrated/Set Number: X84313 TK2 R1 F105/Getty Images, 10–11; David Cannon/David Cannon Collection/Getty Images, 13; Scott Heppell/AP Images, 15; Chatchai Somwat/Shutterstock Images, 16–17; David Goldman/AP Images, 19; Marilyn Indahl/Icon Sportswire, 21; Frank Franklin II/AP Images, 25; Seth Wenig/AP Images, 27; Red Line Editorial, 29

Library of Congress Cataloging-in-Publication Data
Library of Congress Cataloging-in-Publication Data is available on the Library of Congress website.

ISBN
978-1-64493-053-3 (hardcover)
978-1-64493-132-5 (paperback)
978-1-64493-290-2 (ebook pdf)
978-1-64493-211-7 (hosted ebook)

Printed in the United States of America
Mankato, MN
012020

ABOUT THE AUTHOR

Anthony K. Hewson is a freelance writer originally from San Diego, now living in the Bay Area with his wife and their two dogs.

TABLE OF CONTENTS

CHAPTER 1

SLAMMING THE DOOR

Brooks Koepka stood on the green of the 13th hole. All he had left was a 9-foot (2.7-m) putt for **par**. But Koepka knew this one was big. He was playing in the 2017 US Open. And the rest of the golfers were on his heels.

Koepka calmly drew back his club. He struck the ball and watched it roll.

Koepka tees off during the final round of the 2017 US Open.

It dropped right into the center of the cup. The putt gave Koepka a two-stroke lead. But he celebrated with only a slight pump of his fist. He knew there was more work to do.

Most fans thought of Koepka as a big, strong golfer. He was best known for his long drives. But to win his first **major**, he had to be solid on the green.

On the 14th hole, Koepka's second shot landed in the sand trap. It was going to be tough to get the ball close to the hole. But Koepka hit a beautiful shot to within 6 feet (1.8 m). Then he buried the putt.

Next up was the 15th hole, a par 4. Koepka hit a perfect second shot. It

Koepka blasts out of the bunker on the 14th hole.

landed 10 feet (3.0 m) from the cup.

Koepka made his second **birdie** in a row.

Then he moved to the 16th hole, a par 3.

Koepka's tee shot was good, but he left a long putt. It was 17 feet (5.2 m) away from the hole. Koepka's putt started off to the right. But it slowly drifted back to the left. When it dropped into the cup, Koepka made a bigger fist pump.

Meanwhile, the field was fading. By the 18th hole, nobody could catch Koepka.

A RECORD PERFORMANCE

The history of the US Open goes back more than 100 years. But Koepka was just the second person ever to shoot such a low score. His finish at −16 tied Rory McIlroy's mark from 2011. Koepka was only the seventh golfer ever to shoot double digits below par at the Open.

Koepka shows off his trophy after winning the 2017 US Open.

As he made his final short putt, he pumped his fist twice. Koepka was a cool customer. He never got too high or too low. Even in winning his first major, he was all business.

CHAPTER 2

THE ALL-AMERICAN

Brooks Koepka was born on May 3, 1990. Growing up in Florida, Brooks played many sports. He enjoyed baseball, hockey, and basketball. Baseball was his favorite, and golf wasn't really a factor. In fact, young Brooks considered it boring.

When Brooks was 10 years old, he injured his face in a serious car accident.

Koepka takes part in a college championship tournament in 2010.

Doctors told him he couldn't play any contact sports for a while. So Brooks joined his dad, Bob, at the local golf course.

It turned out that Brooks had a talent for the sport. Almost immediately, he was better than his dad. At the age of 13, Brooks beat his dad for the club

BASEBALL FAMILY

Growing up, Brooks Koepka's first sport was baseball. He has said if he wasn't a pro golfer, he would have been a baseball player. The game runs in his family. His dad played baseball in college. And his great-uncle is Dick Groat, who played shortstop for the Pittsburgh Pirates. Groat even won the Most Valuable Player (MVP) award in 1960.

Koepka competes in the 2012 US Open.

championship. Bob Koepka had won it five years in a row.

Brooks was a star in high school and went on to play college golf. He attended Florida State, on the opposite end of the state from his hometown of Lake Worth.

Brooks shined as a college golfer. He was a three-time All-American, meaning he was one of the top golfers in three different years. He was a team captain and set records for scoring average.

By 2012, Brooks was good enough to turn pro. But he didn't start out on the major American tour. Brooks developed his skills on the Challenge Tour in Europe. It taught him about golf and life. He learned to be on his own. And he learned the daily challenges of playing on a pro golf tour.

Brooks won his first event in 2012 and won three more in 2013. He also started to have opportunities to play

Koepka talks to his caddie at the 2013 British Open.

in bigger events. He qualified for the 2012 US Open and 2013 British Open. He missed the **cut** at both. But he kept working, hoping bigger things were ahead.

CHAPTER 3

MAKING THE CUT

Like players in any other sport, golfers have to earn their way to the top. The top is the Professional Golfers Association (PGA) Tour. Players have to qualify for PGA Tour status. If a golfer does well enough in smaller tournaments, he earns his tour card. That qualifies him to compete on the tour.

Koepka launches a tee shot at a tournament in Thailand in 2013.

Brooks Koepka was on his way to earning a PGA Tour card by 2014. An early indication of what he could do came at the US Open that summer. On the 18th hole, Koepka hit a **wedge** shot. It landed within 6 feet (1.8 m) of the hole. He made the putt and finished fourth.

MOTHER'S INSPIRATION

In 2011, Koepka's mother, Denise, learned that she had cancer. In 2012, Koepka was just beginning his pro golf career and was playing far away from home. Being away from his mom was tough. But Denise told her son to keep fighting his battle while she fought hers. She told him to stick it out. Koepka said that was the best advice he ever received. By the end of 2012, Denise was cancer-free.

Koepka lines up a putt at the 2014 US Open.

Back in the clubhouse, Koepka learned that the top four finishers qualify for the next season's Masters tournament. And Koepka had enough points to earn his tour card. He was now a full-time tour pro.

Koepka capped off 2014 with a win on the European Tour. He was named **Rookie** of the Year. He was also nominated for PGA Tour Rookie of the Year. Koepka was no longer just a player from a small tour. Everyone in the golf world was about to learn his name.

The Phoenix Open was one of the first tour events of 2015. Koepka was behind for most of the weekend. But he made a charge on the final day of the tournament. On the 15th hole, he nailed a 50-foot (15-m) putt for an **eagle**. That gave him the lead, and he never looked back. He won his first PGA Tour event with a 5-under 66.

Koepka makes his way out of a sand trap during the 2016 Ryder Cup.

In 2016, Koepka played for his country. He was on the US team that won the Ryder Cup on home soil. It was more proof that he was among the best golfers in the world.

CHAPTER 4

BECOMING NO. 1

Brooks Koepka's breakthrough season ended in a thud. He injured his wrist at a tournament in December 2017. He ended up finishing dead last. Koepka tried playing through the pain. But it wasn't working. He needed surgery. The recovery time forced him to miss the 2018 Masters.

Koepka watches the ball sail during a tournament in 2017.

He hated watching it on TV. He wanted to be out there playing. But he wanted to be sure he was ready for the US Open. After all, he had a title to defend.

Koepka was ready to go for the Open. The course was much tougher than the previous year. There would be no −16 this time. Heading into the final round, Koepka was tied for the lead at +3.

Tommy Fleetwood was right on Koepka's heels. Fleetwood put together an amazing final round. He shot nine under par. But as usual, Koepka stayed calm. Just like he did in 2017, Koepka made his putts down the stretch. He had just one **bogey** on the **back nine**.

Koepka hits out of the rough in the final round of the 2018 US Open.

On hole 16, Koepka got some breathing room. He hit a perfect shot that landed a few feet from the cup. Then he then nailed the putt for a two-shot lead. Nobody could catch him. He became the US Open champ for the second year in a row.

Later that year, he added another major title. And he did it by beating a legend.

Koepka outdueled Tiger Woods at the 2018 PGA Championship. Two months later, a tournament win made Koepka No. 1 in the world golf rankings.

In 2019, Koepka defended his PGA Championship title. But he nearly let it get away. He had a six-shot lead 10 holes

PRO BRO

Brooks Koepka has a younger brother named Chase who is also a pro golfer. Chase is four years younger. Like Brooks, he started his pro career in Europe. As of 2019, he had yet to break onto the American tour. But the brothers have still played together. They were partners at the 2019 Zurich Classic. That tournament is the only tour event with a team format. The brothers finished tied for 22nd.

Koepka pumps his fist after winning the 2019 PGA Championship.

into the final round. However, his friend Dustin Johnson almost caught him. Koepka stayed calm, just like he always does. He held on for a two-shot win.

Koepka had already won four majors, and he was only 29 years old. It took a lot of hard work to get there. But Koepka always bet on himself. Sticking with it had gotten him far.

BROOKS KOEPKA

- Height: 6 feet (183 cm)
- Weight: 205 pounds (93 kg)
- Birth date: May 3, 1990
- Birthplace: West Palm Beach, Florida
- High school: Cardinal Newman High School (West Palm Beach, Florida)
- College: Florida State University (Tallahassee, Florida)
- Major awards: Ryder Cup winner (2016); US Open Champion (2017, 2018); PGA Champion (2018, 2019)

Tallahassee

West Palm Beach

FOCUS ON
BROOKS KOEPKA

Write your answers on a separate piece of paper.

1. Write a letter to a friend describing how Koepka discovered the game of golf.

2. Which of the four majors (Masters, US Open, PGA Championship, or British Open) would you most like to watch? Why?

3. Where did Koepka go to college?
   - **A.** Europe
   - **B.** Florida
   - **C.** Pittsburgh

4. Why did Koepka start his pro career in Europe?
   - **A.** He was not good enough to play on the PGA Tour.
   - **B.** His family lived in Europe, so he wanted to play there.
   - **C.** Europe had better players than the United States.

Answer key on page 32.

GLOSSARY

back nine
Holes 10 through 18 in a round of golf.

birdie
A score of one under par on a golf hole.

bogey
A score of one over par on a golf hole.

cut
When the number of players is reduced in a tournament, leaving only the players with the best scores to play the final rounds.

eagle
A score of two under par on a golf hole.

major
One of the four biggest golf tournaments. They include the Masters, the US Open, the British Open, and the PGA Championship.

par
The score a good golfer should make on a hole.

rookie
A professional athlete in his or her first year.

wedge
A golf club designed to hit the ball high into the air.

TO LEARN MORE

BOOKS

Gitlin, Marty. *Jordan Spieth: Golf Star*. Lake Elmo, MN: Focus Readers, 2017.

Webster, Christine. *The Masters*. New York: AV2 by Weigl, 2018.

Wells, Don. *Golf*. New York: AV2 by Weigl, 2018.

NOTE TO EDUCATORS

Visit **www.focusreaders.com** to find lesson plans, activities, links, and other resources related to this title.

INDEX

Answer Key: **1.** Answers will vary; **2.** Answers will vary; **3.** B; **4.** A